OPERATION EARTH

TROUBLED WATERS

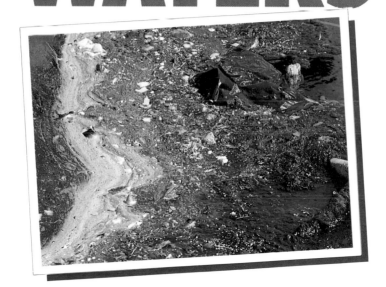

by
Dennis Leggett
and
Jeremy Leggett

A Templar Book
First published in Great Britain in 1991
by Heinemann Children's Reference
A division of Heinemann Educational Books Ltd
Halley Court, Jordan Hill, Oxford OX2 8EJ
Devised and produced by The Templar Company plc
Pippbrook Mill, London Road, Dorking, Surrey RH4 1JE

Editors: Wendy Madgwick, Steve Parker
Designer: Jane Hunt
Illustrator: Rod Ferring

Colour separations by Positive Colour Ltd, Maldon, Essex
Printed and bound by L.E.G.O., Vicenza, Italy

British Library Cataloguing in Publication Data

Leggett, Dennis
Troubled waters.
1. Water. Pollution
I. Title   II. Leggett, Jeremy   III. Series
363.7394

ISBN 0-431-00791-8

Whilst the contents of this book are believed correct at the time of going to
press, changes may have occurred since that time or will occur during
the currency of this book.

Photographic credits
t = top, b = bottom, l = left, r = right, m = middle
Cover: Robert Harding; inset: Ian Griffiths/Robert Harding;
page 6 John Clegg/Ardea; page 8 Goldwater/Network Photographers;
page 12 John and Jenny Hubley; page 15 Tony Morrison; page 19 Gene
Feldman/NASA GSFC/Science Photo Library; page 21 M. Timothy O'Keefe/Bruce
Coleman; page 22 Dr Jeremy Burgess/Science Photo Library; page 24
Edwards/Greenpeace; page 25 Bob Edwards/Science Photo Library; page 26
Sally and Richard Greenhill; page 27 United States Travel and Tourism
Administration; page 30 *l* United States Travel and Tourism Administration;
page 30 *r* H. Gruyart/Telegraph Colour Library; page 32 *l* Fritz Prenzel/Bruce
Coleman; page 32 *r* Vennemann/Greenpeace; page 33 United States Travel and
Tourism Administration; page 35 *t* Mark N. Boulton/Bruce Coleman; page 35 *b*
Zefa; page 36 Morgan/Greenpeace; page 37 Francisco Erize/Bruce Coleman;
page 38 Merjenburgh/Greenpeace; page 39 Spaans/Greenpeace; page 40
Morgan/Greenpeace; page 41 *t* Tony Craddock/Science Photo Library; page 41 *m*
Dorreboom/Greenpeace; page 41 *b* Ian Griffiths/Robert Harding.

CONTENTS

WATER AND LIFE

All living things need water. It is vital for the chemical processes within their bodies. Water permits life. This miraculous substance dissolves many other chemicals and allows them to react together – which is what happens inside the bodies of living things. Water is slow to change temperature. It provides physical protection for many forms of life.

Water moves around our planet from one place to another. This is called the water cycle. Water gets into the air in many ways. For example, it may evaporate from the sea, or evaporate as sweat from an animal, or be released through the leaves of a plant (**transpiration**). In the atmosphere, water vapour condenses into tiny drops that form clouds. It returns to the Earth's surface as rain, hail, snow and dew. Water also comes from within the planet. It is released as steam from hot springs and volcanoes. From all these sources it has built up in rocks over hundreds of thousands of years,

MORE AND MORE WATER

Humans use more water each year. In 1950, global water consumption was 1000 cubic kilometres. By 1980 it was 3500 cubic kilometres, and rising faster than ever. On average, 73% of water is used for irrigation, 22% by industry, and 5% is for domestic use.

A WATERY PLANET
Despite the abundance of water, millions of people are dying or suffering for the want of it. Of all the water on Earth, about 0.01% is clean fresh water that is readily available to humans.

by moving into tiny spaces in rocks called pores. Such water is known as groundwater. Fresh water moves from land to sea each year in rivers and as floodwater.

A human being needs at least 5 litres of water each day for basic survival. A "reasonable" standard of living requires about 80 litres for domestic use. The human population of the world is approaching 6,000 million people. In principle, there should be enough water on Earth for 20,000 million people if it is used sensibly, but it isn't. A great deal of water is wasted. We are also reducing the amount of useable water by dirtying it and poisoning it with pollutants. This book explains how water is being wasted and polluted, and how we can help to save water and use it more carefully.

WATER USAGE
People in different places use different amounts of water. Millions of people in developing countries have barely enough water to survive, while people in developed countries waste dozens of litres daily.

THE WATER CYCLE
Water is always on the move. It is continuously recycled, as it falls from the sky, filters through the soil, and rises into the atmosphere as vapour. This diagram shows the main paths in the water cycle.

**New York City, USA
300 litres daily**

**Nigeria
120 litres daily**

**India
25 litres daily**

**Madagascar
5.4 litres daily**

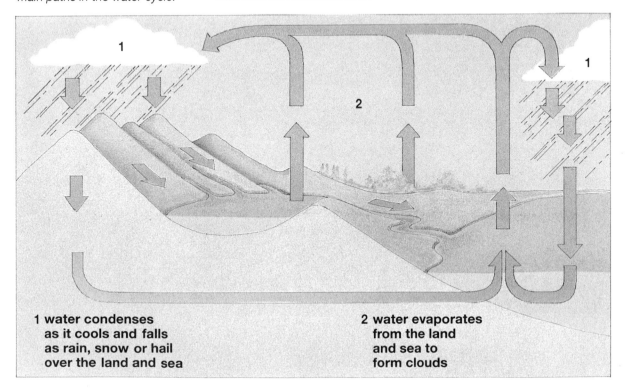

**1 water condenses
as it cools and falls
as rain, snow or hail
over the land and sea**

**2 water evaporates
from the land
and sea to
form clouds**

A WATERY WORLD

Although our planet is called the Earth, almost three-quarters of its surface is covered by water. This water is distributed very unevenly. Almost all of it, more than 97 per cent, is in the oceans. This means that all other water – in ice caps and glaciers, groundwater in the rocks, fresh water in lakes and rivers, water vapour in the air, droplets in clouds, and water in the soil and the bodies of all living things – is less than one-thirtieth of the total.

Water is returned to land by the various forms of **precipitation**, such as rain, hail, snow and dew. As we all know, rain falls very unevenly around the world. Some areas receive a lot, others very little. People are also spread unevenly. Increasingly, they live in cities. A growing number of cities have populations of more than 10 million. It is not easy to provide clean water for so many people crowded into such a small place.

DEVASTATING DROUGHT
Ethiopia has suffered many droughts (see below). Only 100 millimetres of rain falls in some areas each year. In the early 1980s, vast areas of crops were ruined and millions of farm animals died in the droughts.

In areas liable to drought, people find it difficult to feed themselves. There is famine if the rains do not arrive and sometimes sources of water dry up completely. This has happened in recent years in the Sahel region of Africa (see page 10), including Ethiopia and the Sudan.

Another strain on water resources is our demand for goods and services. A person living in an industrialized country uses huge amounts of water indirectly. This "hidden" use of water amounts to much more than the volume we use directly.

WATER USED IN ONE DAY

These figures show the typical amounts of water used each day by a person in a developed country such as the USA. As you can see, most of the use is "indirect". Many of these uses could be cut down.

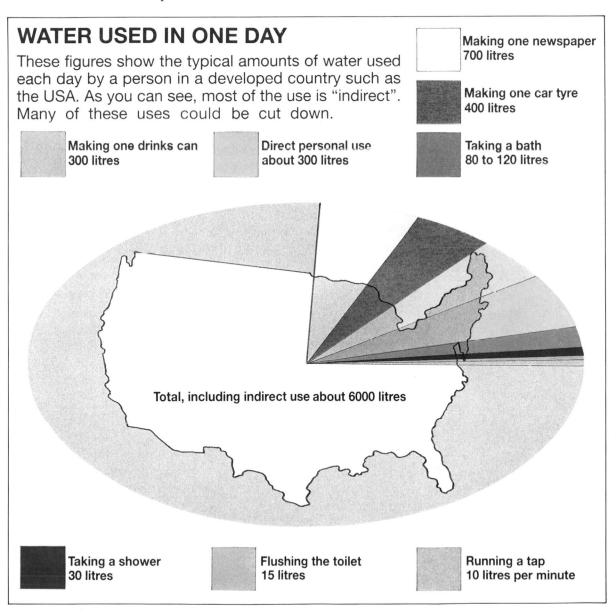

Making one newspaper
700 litres

Making one car tyre
400 litres

Taking a bath
80 to 120 litres

Making one drinks can
300 litres

Direct personal use
about 300 litres

Total, including indirect use about 6000 litres

Taking a shower
30 litres

Flushing the toilet
15 litres

Running a tap
10 litres per minute

DISAPPEARING WATER

BETTER IRRIGATION

There is much scope to increase the efficiency of irrigation around the world. Nearly three-quarters of all water used by humans is intended for irrigation. However, inefficient methods mean that only 37% of this irrigation water is actually taken up by plants. New developments in irrigation techniques will save huge quantities of water.

Satellites and astronauts take photographs that tell us what is happening on the surface of our Earth. The photographs can be combined with measurements on the ground to identify areas where starvation is likely if rains or food crops fail. In Africa, millions of people live with the threat of starvation. If the already-low rainfall is reduced for some reason, the result is disaster. The area south of the Sahara Desert, named the Sahel, is a tragic example of this.

Photographs taken on the US Gemini 6 space mission, in 1965, showed an area of the Sahel called the inland Niger delta. It was rich in lakes and vegetation. A band of grassland about 200 kilometres wide stretched northwards to the Sahara. Satellite

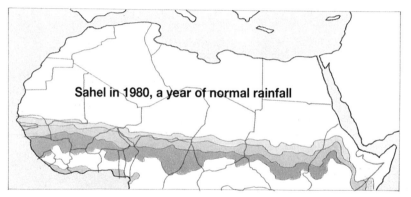

Sahel in 1984, a year of drought

Desert moves south

Sahel in 1980, a year of normal rainfall

KEY

Vegetation zone

- little or no vegetation
- moderate vegetation
- heavy vegetation
- Sahara region

DROUGHT IN THE SAHEL
During the 1950s and 1960s, the Sahel region had more rain than usual. Vast areas were newly cultivated – not to grow food, but to raise mainly cash crops for sale to developed countries. People and their animals had to move north to the new grasslands at the desert edge. In the 1970s and 1980s drought struck. The grasslands turned to desert. Millions died, and the edge of the Sahara moved southwards.

photographs of the same area in 1985 showed no grass, few lakes and little vegetation.

Farther east, in another area of the Sahel, lies the great Lake Chad. Satellite pictures from 1966 showed the lake to have 22,000 square kilometres of open water, dotted with islands. There were villages on many of the islands. The people lived by fishing and growing corn. Yet by 1985, the photographs revealed that the lake had shrunk to only one-fifth of its previous size. The people's way of life was destroyed.

Now, the United Nations Food and Agriculture Organization receive weekly satellite reports on the Sahel. These are combined with measurements of rainfall and crop yields. The results help to forecast drought and starvation. Then food supplies can be arranged to lessen the impact of the famine.

The problem of water supply for agriculture could get worse. The **greenhouse effect** is produced by "greenhouse gases" such as carbon dioxide being put into the atmosphere by industry, transport and agriculture. Computer forecasts show that, in the coming decades, there could be less rainfall and more drought in tropical areas. Industrialized countries would be called on to give even more aid to tropical countries, most of which are already poor.

THE GREENHOUSE EFFECT
Greenhouse gases act like a blanket around the Earth. They let the Sun's rays in, but they stop heat passing out into space. Unless we cut the greenhouse gases we produce, the greenhouse effect will cause global warming, and gradually make the world's climate hotter. The climate would also become drier in many tropical and subtropical regions. This is described in more detail in the Air Scare book in this series.

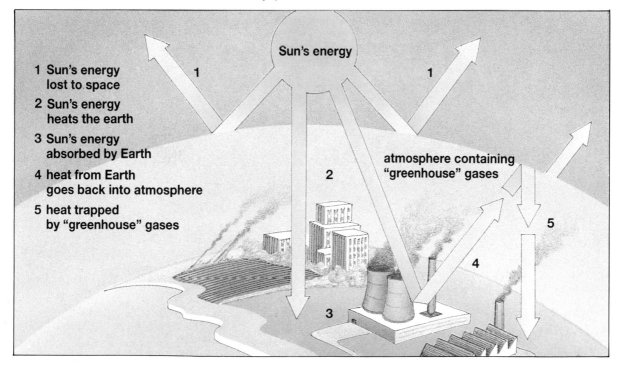

Sun's energy

1 Sun's energy lost to space

2 Sun's energy heats the earth

3 Sun's energy absorbed by Earth

4 heat from Earth goes back into atmosphere

5 heat trapped by "greenhouse" gases

atmosphere containing "greenhouse" gases

CLEAN, SAFE WATER

About one-third of all people on our planet lack clean, safe water. Over half of all people have no safe means for sanitation. Lack of safe water and proper sanitation cause three-quarters of all illnesses in developing countries. Even in industrialized countries, some rural areas and city slums do not have a good supply of clean water.

Many dangerous diseases are carried in water or spread by snails, insects and other animals that live in water. Diseases involving diarrhoea are often caused by contaminated water. These diseases are among the biggest killers of children under five, especially in developing countries. Diarrhoea causes loss of body water and so **dehydration**. Over 3,500,000 children die of dehydration every year in developing countries.

IS IT SAFE?
It is impossible to tell whether water is clean and pure simply by looking at it. Millions of people struggle daily to find clean water for cooking and drinking. Dried milk is still supplied by companies in developed countries to African hospitals, where mothers are taught to bottle feed their babies. When they go home, there is no clean water to make up the milk nor clean the bottles. If the water is not clean, the babies can become very ill.

Clean, safe water is needed for many other reasons. It is important for good hygiene during birth, and for medical treatments of all kinds. It is vital for food and drink. Babies can become ill if their feeding bottles have been "cleaned" in unsterilized water.

Water is essential for producing food crops. If there is not enough rain, crops can be watered to make them grow by a process called **irrigation**. Water is taken from rivers, lakes or the ground for this purpose. Worldwide, an area of land the size of India is irrigated. About seven-tenths of the world's fresh water supplies is used for irrigation.

If land is overwatered by irrigation, problems arise. In hotter climates much of the water quickly evaporates, leaving behind deposits of salt (salination) or soda (sodification). This poisons or contaminates the soil. Today, of 270 million hectares of land under irrigation, some 60-80 million hectares are affected by salination.

TOO MUCH IRRIGATION

Putting extra water on the land helps crops to grow. Yet too much irrigation causes salination, when salt builds up in the soil. Up to 30 million hectares of irrigated land suffer so badly from salination that they are becoming unusable. Even in a rich country such as the USA, 20% of irrigated land is salinated.

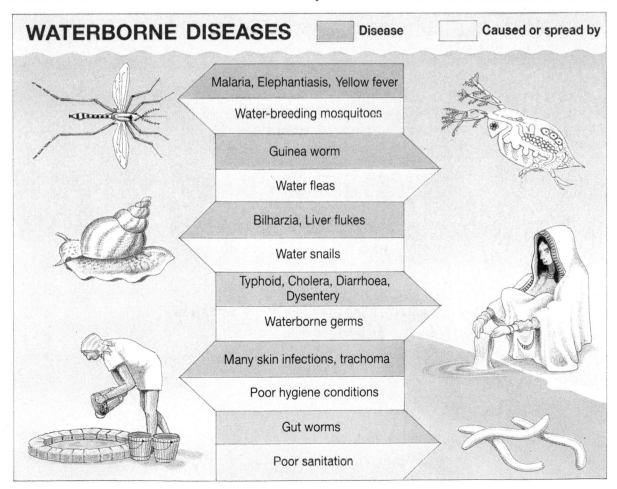

WATERBORNE DISEASES

| | Disease | | Caused or spread by |

Malaria, Elephantiasis, Yellow fever

Water-breeding mosquitoes

Guinea worm

Water fleas

Bilharzia, Liver flukes

Water snails

Typhoid, Cholera, Diarrhoea, Dysentery

Waterborne germs

Many skin infections, trachoma

Poor hygiene conditions

Gut worms

Poor sanitation

FRESH WATER

Living things form a web of life. Different types of animals and plants are adapted to each type of watery environment, from puddles to ponds and lakes, from streams to rivers, and from the edge of the sea to the open ocean's surface and dark depths.

The inhabitants of each type of watery world become adjusted to conditions there. The temperature of the water, the amount of light, the levels of oxygen, **nutrients** (chemicals needed for plant growth) and acidity as well as water movement are all important. If just one of these factors is upset, the delicate balance of life can be ruined.

As water flows to the sea, it changes greatly. Young streams in the hills are fast-flowing. Here the animals cling to rocks or swim very strongly, and they rely on lots of oxygen dissolved in the water. Plants must be anchored securely, away from the fastest current.

THE LIFE OF A RIVER
If you travel along a healthy river, the animals and plants gradually change with the water conditions.
1. Trout and mayfly larvae thrive in the upper reaches.
2. Various fish, great diving beetles and water boatmen live along the middle stretches.
3. In the lower reaches above sea level are marsh plants, tall reeds and water lilies, and fish like carp.

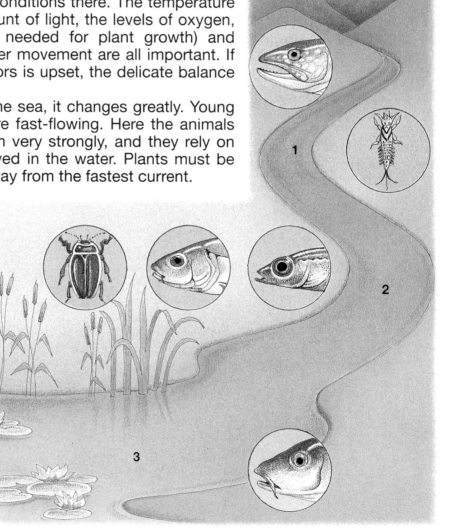

DEAD WATERS

The River Rother, in Yorkshire, England, is almost a "dead" river. Water plants and fish, insects and many other creatures can no longer live in 60% of it or along its banks. The fish have all been killed by heavy pollution from industries along a 30-kilometre stretch.

In the USA, Lake Erie, once a "dead" lake due to toxic sewage pollution, is being cleaned up. Plant and animal life is returning, although water sports are still restricted along stretches of its shore and fish taken from the lake are often unfit as food. It is estimated that using current anti-pollution measures it will be 75 years before the lake is safe.

Many lakes affected by **acid rain** look deceptively clean because their waters are so clear. However, the water is clear because it is too acidic for life. In a healthy lake, it would be tinted by growths of plants and the tiny animals swimming in it.

The middle reaches of a river have fast stretches and pools. There is a little less oxygen in the water, but many more swimming animals. The river's lower reaches contain even less oxygen, and the water is slow-moving and murky. Yet it is still home to many different types of animals and plants.

Lakes vary, too. Many mountain lakes are deep and steep-sided. They tend to have high levels of oxygen but not a great variety of life, because the water lacks nutrients. Lakes that have shallow edges, and are high in plant nutrients, have many more life forms.

However, rivers and lakes are used as dumps by industry. Wastes, chemicals and many other harmful substances are poured into them. The balance of nature is upset. Plants and animals sicken and die.

COASTAL WATERS

The edges of the seas are often rich in animal and plant life. People have always used this environment to fish, hunt animals and gather plants. More than half of all humans live in coastal regions.

River estuaries and deltas are particularly rich in life, but they are also the sites for ports and towns, and so they suffer pollution. The diagram opposite shows the sources and types of pollution.

For instance, oil escapes accidentally from refineries and oil tankers. It is also released deliberately, but illegally, by ships at sea. In small amounts, oil can be broken down by bacteria in the water. In large amounts, it damages animals and plants, as well as making a mess of beaches.

Dangerous chemicals like dioxins, polychlorinated biphenyls (**PCBs**) and heavy metals build up in food chains. For example, shellfish take in PCBs carried in the water, with their food. Animals that eat the shellfish gradually build up the toxins in their bodies, especially in fat tissues. This is called **bio-accumulation**. PCBs, for example, can become concentrated in the fat of some sea mammals, to levels 80 million times higher than in the surrounding water. If these animals are then eaten by people, they too can be poisoned.

Sewage pollution and agricultural run-off speed up eutrophication in coastal waters (see pages 22–26). The effects can be disastrous. In Chesapeake Bay, USA, the crabs, oysters and fish are disappearing as a result of the mixture of industrial and agricultural pollutants being discharged into the bay. As the animals disappear, whole fishing communities have lost their livelihood.

Like rivers, coasts can be recovered. In the past 10 years, some North American and European coasts have begun to show a drop in pollution. Marine parks and protected coastal areas are being set up in different parts of the world (see page 20).

COASTAL POLLUTION

● Agricultural run-off. Fertilizers, pesticides and other chemicals run-off into the sea.
● Nuclear industry. Low-level radioactive waste, and thermal pollution from the cooling water needed by power stations discharge from inshore pipes.
● Oil spills and discharges. Oil refineries are often built on the coast, where the crude oil is unloaded from large oil tankers or undersea pipelines.
● Industrial contamination. Many coastal cities have large industries, with easy sea access for imports and exports.
● Tourism. Too many people contribute to the sewage and refuse problem.

A DEAD DELTA

A dead zone in the delta of the River Mississipi, USA covers about 0.9 million hectares it is growing by about 20% a year and is probably due to run-off of nitrates. In 1987, sediments from the Gulf of Mexico suggested toxic waste came from off-shore oil wells, industry and the air. Despite the dead zone and heavy metal contamination of sea animals, there is no Federal monitoring of the pollution.

ESTUARY PROBLEMS

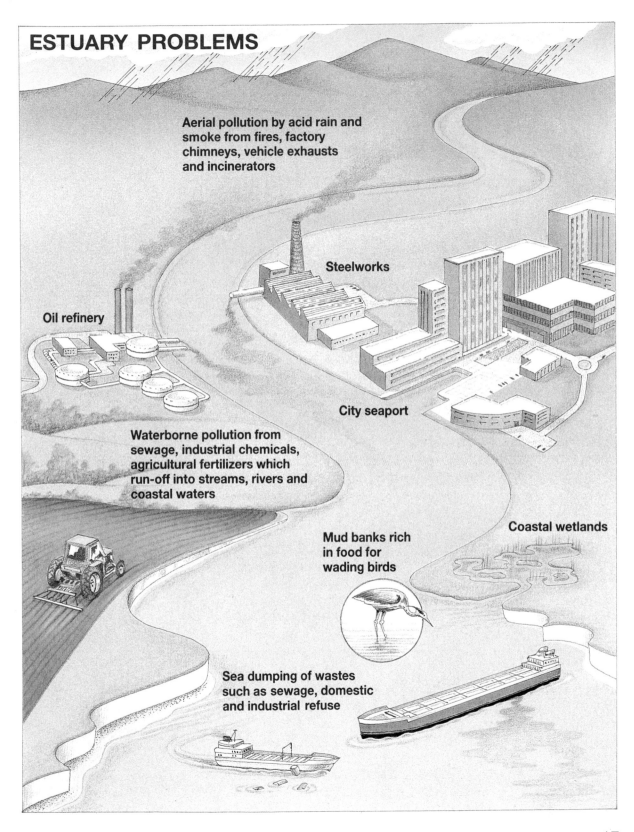

Aerial pollution by acid rain and smoke from fires, factory chimneys, vehicle exhausts and incinerators

Steelworks

Oil refinery

City seaport

Waterborne pollution from sewage, industrial chemicals, agricultural fertilizers which run-off into streams, rivers and coastal waters

Coastal wetlands

Mud banks rich in food for wading birds

Sea dumping of wastes such as sewage, domestic and industrial refuse

SEAS AND OCEANS

THE OCEAN FROM SPACE
In this satellite photograph (right), a computer has colour-coded the different areas. In the oceans the reds and yellows pick out regions of "productivity", where the algae grow well and provide food for many animals. Pink and blue areas have least growth. The land masses are shown as dark green (dense vegetation) to pale yellow (little vegetation).

The richness and variety of life in the sea varies greatly, from one area to another. Coastal waters and the shallow continental shelf regions, around the main land masses, support the most life.

Coastal waters are fed by rivers bringing nutrients from the land. The nutrients are taken up by micro-scopic plants that float near the surface. Sunlight can penetrate about 100 metres below the sea's surface. Nearer the surface, the microscopic plants take in light energy and use it to grow and make food, in the process called photosynthesis .

FOOD CHAINS OF THE OCEAN

At the base of a food chain are the plants. On land, the plants are familiar trees, grasses and flowers. In the open ocean, the plants are mostly microscopic relatives of the seaweeds.

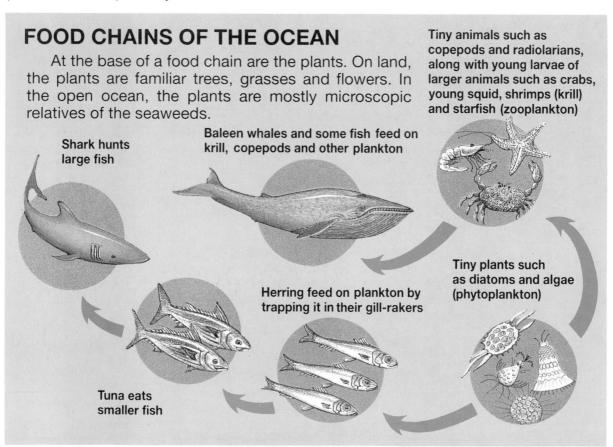

Tiny animals such as copepods and radiolarians, along with young larvae of larger animals such as crabs, young squid, shrimps (krill) and starfish (zooplankton)

Shark hunts large fish

Baleen whales and some fish feed on krill, copepods and other plankton

Tiny plants such as diatoms and algae (phytoplankton)

Herring feed on plankton by trapping it in their gill-rakers

Tuna eats smaller fish

18

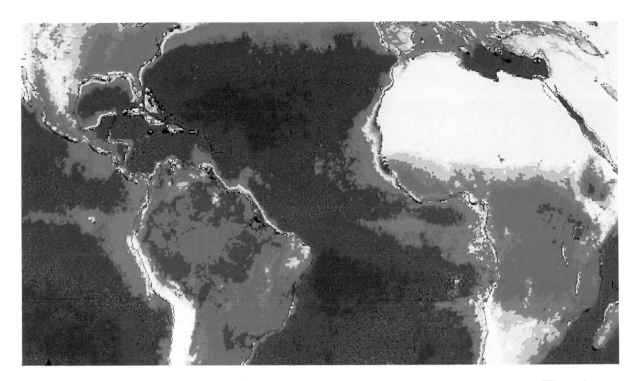

LIVING IN LEVELS

Most sea creatures live at a certain level in the water. The euphotic zone consists of the upper layer where light can penetrate, allowing plants to grow. The pelagic area makes up the main body of a sea or lake. The benthic area is the lower and bottom level.

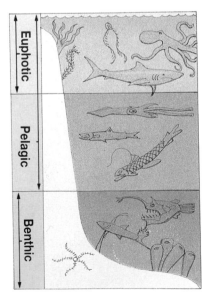

The tiny plants are eaten by tiny animals. The plants and tiny animals are together called plankton. Larger creatures feed on the plankton, and they in turn are eaten by larger ones, and so on. The chain of small plants being eaten by small animals, which are eaten by ever bigger animals, is called a food chain.

In coastal waters, seaweeds also carry out photo-synthesis. They give shelter as well as food to animals. At the sea's edges are areas such as mangrove swamps, saltmarshes, river estuaries and coral reefs. These places are very rich in plants and animals. A huge proportion of the millions of different living things (species) on our planet dwell in just two environments: tropical rainforests and coral reefs.

The rich coasts and continental shelves make up only about one-twelfth of the area of the oceans. The continental slopes, which dip into deeper water, occupy twice that area. Nearly all of the rest of the oceans is made up of the abyssal plain. Here the water averages several kilometres in depth. At this depth there are no plants because it is too dark, and so there are fewer fish and other animals.

In many places, life in the sea is under threat from humans. The two main threats are pollution (see pages 22–29) and overfishing (see page 30).

CORAL REEFS

Coral reefs abound with life. About one-third of all the different species of fish known live there. The coral animals live in colonies, and their chalky skeletons form the rock of the reef. Some types of coral build the reef base and main structure, while others fill it in. As the reef grows, the corals die and others grow on top.

New scientific discoveries about life on coral reefs are being made all the time. For example, some reef inhabitants make substances, such as histamines and antibiotics, that are useful as medicines for humans. We do not yet know of all the benefits that coral reefs might provide – if they were managed properly.

Coral reefs are not being managed properly. In many parts of the world, human activities are destroying reefs.

PROTECTED IN NAME ONLY

The governments of the Caribbean have named 112 marine parks and protected areas. However, many of the park authorities do not have enough funds to do their job. Only 25% of the parks have staff and money. Yet the parks that are managed properly show great benefits, both now and for the future:

● Pollution and overfishing are prevented.
● Tourism and local employment increase.
● The parks, with their wildlife, are preserved for the future.

THE GREAT BARRIER REEF

This vast coral reef is 2000 kilometres long, and covers more than 350,000 square kilometres. It is home to more than 3000 animal species, and most of it is a protected marine park. Industry in the area, including tourism, is strictly controlled.

Australia

Queensland

Brisbane●

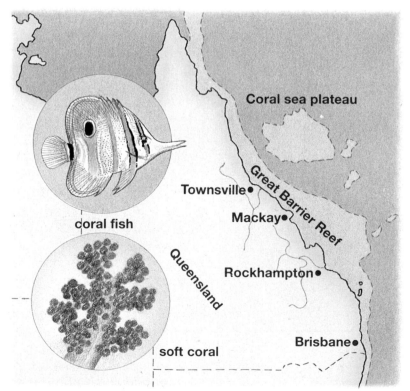

coral fish

soft coral

Coral sea plateau

Townsville●

Mackay●

Great Barrier Reef

Queensland

Rockhampton●

Brisbane●

They are being mined for phosphates. Divers remove ornate shells and rare corals, which they sell to tourists. Fishermen clear the reefs of fish. In the process, nets snag and pull at the corals, damaging them.

The Philippines relies on its coral reefs for one-tenth of its fish catch. Yet the reefs are being damaged and catches are falling. America's only coral reef is off the coast of Florida. Scientists report that large areas of it are dying.

Marine parks and protected areas are designed to do for the sea what national parks and reservations do for the land. They are areas which are managed to maintain the balance of nature. The world's largest coral reef is the Great Barrier Reef, off the north-east coast of Australia. In the 1970s, it seemed that tourists, builders and miners would destroy it. The Marine Park Authority was formed and in 1980, a large portion of the reef was declared a marine park.

The Authority manages the reef in zones. Some zones allow no activities at all; others are kept for research. In other zones there is fishing, and tourist cruises and dives, but these are controlled to preserve the reef. Mining is forbidden. The Authority can even obtain powers to control pollution from outside its boundaries if it threatens the reef.

WHAT IS CORAL?

Corals are very small animals, cousins of jellyfish and sea anemones. Each one lives inside a chalky tube- or cup-shaped skeleton that it makes for itself. Microscopic plants called zooxanthellae (see below) live in partnership with the coral, inside its body. They use light to make food for both themselves and the coral, while the coral supplies nutrients and shelter. The need for light means corals can only grow in shallow, brightly lit waters.

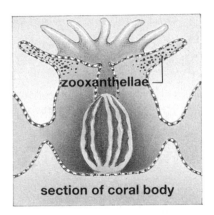

zooxanthellae

section of coral body

TOO MUCH FERTILIZER

Many fish and other water creatures depend on microscopic algae that live in the surface waters of lakes, rivers and seas. As the algae die and sink through the water, bacteria break down their bodies. As they do this, the bacteria use up oxygen dissolved in the water.

Under certain conditions, and usually in lakes, the algae grow very quickly in the surface waters. As they die and sink, the bacteria that break them down use more and more oxygen. This means there is less and less oxygen in the water for fish and other animals. The bacteria thrive while animals suffer and die. Finally only fungi and some bacteria survive.

Algae grow too fast when nutrients in the lake increase. This is called **eutrophication**. The nutrients come from the chemicals in fertilizers which have been put on fields to make crops grow, and from detergents. Nitrates and phosphates in the fertilizers trickle from

ORGANIC FARMING

A growing number of farmers are changing to natural or organic fertilizers. This involves putting compost from farm animals and humans on the land. A recent study by the US National Academy of Sciences shows that, done properly, organic farming is just as productive as farming with chemically-made fertilizers.

BLOOMING ALGAE
The luxuriant green growths of algae in a pond or lake may look natural and healthy. However, the algal "bloom" is caused by too many nutrients in the water, as a result of fertilizer run-off. The oxygen in the water is used up and fish and other animals die.

farmers' fields into streams and rivers, and so find their way into lakes. These solutions are known as "run-off". Very many lakes in the United States, Canada and Europe suffer eutrophication. Seas that suffer include the North Sea.

High nitrate levels can affect humans, too. Nitrates from fertilizers seep through the ground into supplies of drinking water, whether above ground in rivers or reservoirs, or in wells. Too much nitrate in drinking water can affect the blood of bottle-fed babies, even if the water is boiled. This type of blood disease is rare but increasing. Some scientists believe that there may also be an increased risk of stomach cancer if people drink water high in nitrates.

Run-off through rocks and soils can also come from dumps of domestic and industrial waste, or from spillage. As drums of chemicals rust and as rubbish rots, poisons are released. These dissolve in soil water and find their way into rivers and lakes. They also threaten our drinking water.

TOO MUCH NITRATE

Developed countries are more likely to have high water nitrate levels than developing countries, because they use more fertilizer. Up to 10% of wells sampled in Europe and the USA have nitrate levels that are higher than is generally thought to be safe. Nitrates are also polluting the oceans, as shown on this map. They encourage the growth of algae at the expense of other sea life. In the North Sea, currents and winds concentrate the algal growth on the eastern side.

POTENTIAL ILLNESS

Run-off from fertilizers, pesticides and other chemicals in tap water can pose a health hazard. These are some of the possible problems.

△ **Lead**
Damages the brain, especially in children

☐ **Pesticides**
May cause cancers

○ **Nitrates**
May cause stomach cancer

◇ **Trihalomethanes**
May cause cancers of the bladder, colon and rectum

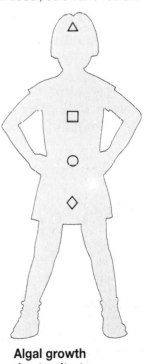

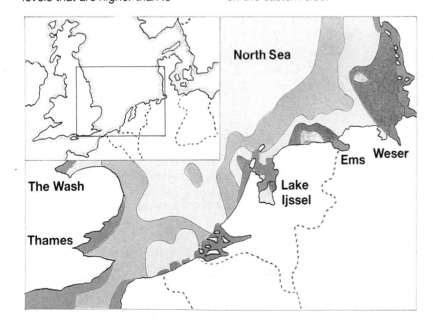

North Sea

Ems Weser

The Wash

Lake Ijssel

Thames

Algal growth due to nitrates

very high
high
moderate
low
almost none

POISONED WATERS

Drains from factories, farms, sewage works and other industrial sites discharge their contents into rivers and lakes. The discharges may be toxic (poisonous and harmful) or non-toxic. Many toxic substances persist in the environment. Once in rivers, they are carried to pollute the sea, too.

Toxic wastes reach rivers and lakes directly from factory discharges, or indirectly from factory chimneys. They are also found in sewage in countries such as Britain and the United States, where industry is allowed to discharge toxic wastes into the sewer system. The most dangerous toxins are heavy metals, various chemicals that contain chlorine, and radioactive wastes. They are very difficult to remove from water. These toxins are taken in by plants and small animals, and then absorbed in greater concentrations by the larger animals that eat them (see page 16).

RIVERS OF WASTE

Nationwide 60,000 industries discharge their waste water directly in to American rivers and lakes at the rate of 70,000 million litres a day. Another 130,000 factories send waste water into sewage systems at about 75,000 million litres a day.

LAKE SUPERIOR

Surface water near the mouth of Blackbird Creek, Lake Superior in the USA, changes from clear to brownish-black due to pollution from a pulp factory. The water smells of sulphur and steam rises from it. The river is covered with foam, so screens are placed across the river to stop the foam from passing into the lake. The lake is protected, but only from unsightly foam.

DUMPED IN THE RIVER
Big chemical plants like the one shown left discharge huge amounts of chemical waste directly into rivers. Levels of mercury and cadmium in the waste are limited by law, but other chemicals, known to be poisonous, are not. These include toluene, xylene and benzene, all of which can cause cancer.

TOXINS IN OUR WATERS

There are many thousands of chemicals in regular use by industry. In Europe, Britain puts controls on just 37 and the Rhine countries list 40. The European Community lists 129 chemicals needing control.

Heavy metals such as zinc, chromium, nickel. They are used in industrial processes such as the manufacture of fungicides, batteries, paint, petrol, steel and electroplating.

Chlorine compounds such as pesticides, PCBs, **HHCs** and dioxins. They are used in industrial processes such as the manufacture of solvents, plastics, pesticides and bleached paper.

Other chemicals such as organo-phosphates. They are used in manufacture of pesticides. Unlike heavy metals and chlorine compounds, these do not persist in the environment, but they are poisonous.

THE DIRTY SEA
Much of the toxic material in the North Sea comes from Europe's main rivers. Other toxins are dumped directly from ships or burned by incinerator ships. Still others come from inshore pipelines. Here fly ash waste from a coal-fired power station is being loaded on to a ship. It will be dumped into the North Sea.

SEWAGE POLLUTION

Sewage is the waste from animals, including humans. It comes from sewers, manure heaps, cattle yards and slaughter houses. In small amounts, and not polluted with toxic chemicals, it is naturally purified and recycled in lakes, rivers and the sea. Bacteria use oxygen to break down the sewage into a dark "soil" that settles to the bottom of the river or sea, and feeds plants and animals there. However, if sewage is not treated, or if it is too concentrated, it is a risk. In particular, it can kill rivers.

If raw sewage is let into a river or lake, bacteria use it for food. They multiply and use up nearly all the

YOU CAN HELP

Phosphates from cleaners and detergents, such as washing-up liquids, get into sewage. They cause eutrophication in rivers, sea and lakes. Realizing this, many companies now sell environment-friendly, phosphate-free cleaning products. You can help by buying these products, and using the smallest amounts possible.

CHICAGO

Around 1900, Chicago's sewage discharge was redirected to the River Illinois. Now some 6000 industries discharge through the sewers into the river, polluting it with a variety of chemicals. Pesticide and fertilizer run-off also contaminates the river. In 1908, 10% of the United States fresh water fish harvest came from the river. In 1976 it was 0.32%.

SEWAGE TREATMENT
A sewage treatment works speeds up the natural process of sewage recycling. The "soil" is collected (see left) and the water is released into the river. If a sewage works is too old, or poorly designed, it may not be able to deal with all the sewage sent to it. In Britain in 1987, 20% of all inland sewage works dumped raw sewage illegally into rivers.

oxygen in the water. Plants are smothered by the sewage and die. Water animals run short of oxygen and food. Bacteria that can live without oxygen take over, producing foul gases that smell like rotten eggs. The river becomes grey and has slimy, smelly banks.

If the river is long enough or the lake is large enough, it may recover. We can help by making more effort to deal with sewage. For example, in the 1960s Lake Washington, in the USA, was dying. Sewage treatment plants have helped the lake to revive and it is now flourishing.

In many countries, sewage sludge is turned into natural fertilizer for use on fields. All sewage sludge could be used in this way – provided that industry stopped emptying toxic wastes into the sewers. Sewage polluted with poisons cannot be put on fields, since it would contaminate crops and animals.

Sewage is also burned in incinerators in many countries, or buried in landfills. If it contains toxins, however, then these get into the incinerator smoke, or seep into the groundwater from landfills. Scandinavian countries wish to keep industrial wastes out of the sewers. Then the sewage could be burned or used as fertilizer instead of being discharged.

POISONING THE SEA

Although some beaches are well cared for and look beautiful like the long beach peninsula of southwest Washington shown here, many are polluted because raw sewage from nearby towns is dumped straight in the sea. For example, off the New York/New Jersey coast in the USA, an area covering 2704 square kilometres is dead due to sewage discharge. Shellfish within a 10 kilometre radius of the area have been declared dangerous to eat. Similar situations occur in many other areas of the world.

ACID RAIN

Imagine going out in the rain and finding that it tastes as acidic as vinegar. Think what it would do to trees and other plants, or to the health of animals which are outdoors all the time. Yet in many parts of the world, including Europe and North America, there are regular showers of polluted rain which is almost as acidic as weak vinegar.

Rivers and lakes vary in their ability to deal with acid rain. Some are able to absorb it without turning acidic themselves. Others become acidic within a few years. It depends largely on the composition of the soil in the area. Soils that are chalky are resistant to becoming acidic. Clay soils are not.

TRAVELLING ACIDS

Wind blows the acidic fumes and clouds far from the areas where they were produced. In Europe, acid rain is blown to Scandinavia by the prevailing winds from several places: Britain, Germany, and the industrial areas of Eastern Europe and the USSR. In the USA, prevailing winds carry acid rain to Canada, damaging trees and poisoning rivers and lakes. The acid-producers and those who suffer from acid rain, disagree over who should pay for the clean-up.

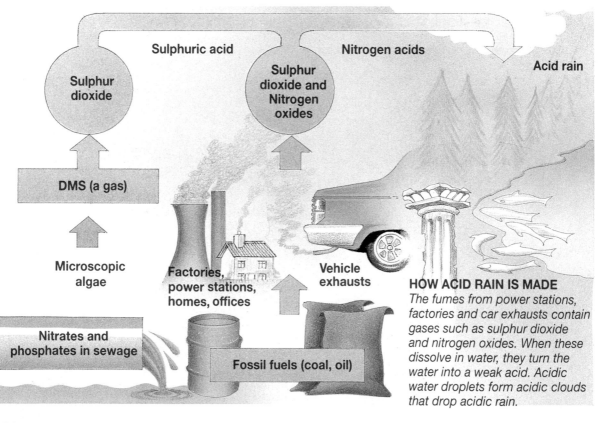

Sulphuric acid

Nitrogen acids

Acid rain

Sulphur dioxide

Sulphur dioxide and Nitrogen oxides

DMS (a gas)

Microscopic algae

Factories, power stations, homes, offices

Vehicle exhausts

Nitrates and phosphates in sewage

Fossil fuels (coal, oil)

HOW ACID RAIN IS MADE
The fumes from power stations, factories and car exhausts contain gases such as sulphur dioxide and nitrogen oxides. When these dissolve in water, they turn the water into a weak acid. Acidic water droplets form acidic clouds that drop acidic rain.

One of the first signs of acidity is that fish such as trout and salmon disappear. When acid rain runs into soil, it dissolves metals from the soil. These pass into the run-off water. One of the metals is aluminium, which damages the gills of fish. Acid rain also damages trees, especially conifers. They lose their leaves and have greater difficulty in taking up water through their roots.

Canada and some European countries have recorded heavy damage due to acid rain. In Sweden, about 20,000 lakes have died (see page 14). In eastern Canada there are 350,000 acidified lakes. The Swedes blame countries like Britain, Germany and Poland for their troubles. The Canadians blame the USA.

Efforts are being made to cut down acid rain. There are two main methods. One is to put filters on power stations, to cut down the gases that make acid rain – sulphur dioxide and nitrogen oxides. The second is to fit vehicle exhausts with filters called catalytic converters, which cut down the acidifying gases. European countries have agreed to reduce both power station and car fumes within a few years. Many scientists argue that much bigger reductions are needed.

ACID COSTS

In 1989 the Canadian Prime Minister reported that acid rain had killed all the fish in 15,000 Canadian lakes. About 300,000 other lakes are threatened.

President Reagan agreed to control nitrogen oxide emission, keeping it at 1987 levels.

HOW RIVER LIFE REACTS

Acidity is measured on the pH scale. Normal life goes on in water of about pH 7, which is neither acidic nor alkaline, but neutral. As water becomes acidic, its pH falls. This is how river life reacts to increasing acidity.

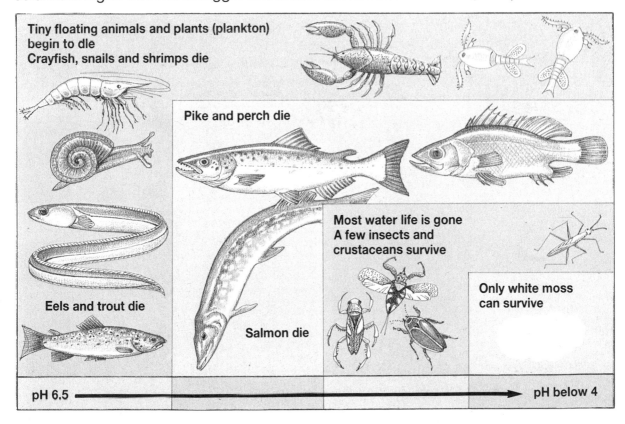

Tiny floating animals and plants (plankton) begin to die
Crayfish, snails and shrimps die

Pike and perch die

Most water life is gone
A few insects and crustaceans survive

Only white moss can survive

Eels and trout die

Salmon die

pH 6.5 ⟶ pH below 4

FISH AND FISHING

In 1950, all the fish people caught from the sea weighed 21 million tonnes. Each year from then, the catch increased. By 1970, it reached more than 70 million tonnes. Since then, however, it has risen no further. There are fewer and fewer fish. The reason is that people have over-fished the seas.

What is more, the type of catch is changing. In 1965, 250,000 tonnes of haddock were caught in the North West Atlantic. In 1974, the catch was only 20,000 tonnes. Herring catches in the North Sea used to be four times bigger than they are today.

Fish catches are used for human food, farm animal feed and fertilizers. About one-third of all fish caught is made into animal feed and fertilizer. This is an extremely wasteful use of the protein packed into fish. One tonne of fishmeal, fed to farm animals, provides less than half a tonne of animal meat. Also, most fish catches go to industrialized countries. Meanwhile, many coastal peoples in poorer countries go hungry.

FISHING METHODS
In some countries, commercial fishing is still done from small fishing boats like these off Alaska (left). In other cases, huge factory ships are used (right). Tonnes of fish are caught and immediately deep frozen or turned into fishmeal.

These days, fishing boats can operate thousands of kilometres from their home port. Their fishing methods are so efficient that they literally clear the seas of fish. They use electronic methods to track fish shoals, and they spread nets so big, with mesh so fine, that they catch all the fish in an area. Driftnets, in particular, are terribly wasteful. When the nets are pulled in, they contain unwanted species, and fish of all ages, even the young that could be left to grow into edible adults. They also trap and drown dolphins and porpoises.

Can we keep this up? The answer is no. The fish populations cannot cope. Fishing must be managed better worldwide.

WHAT DO WE CATCH?
The fish we catch are either bottom-living (demersal) or "free-swimming" (pelagic). Other sea animals caught for food include "shellfish" such as mussels, oysters and crabs. These are not true fish. They belong to other animal groups, as shown here.

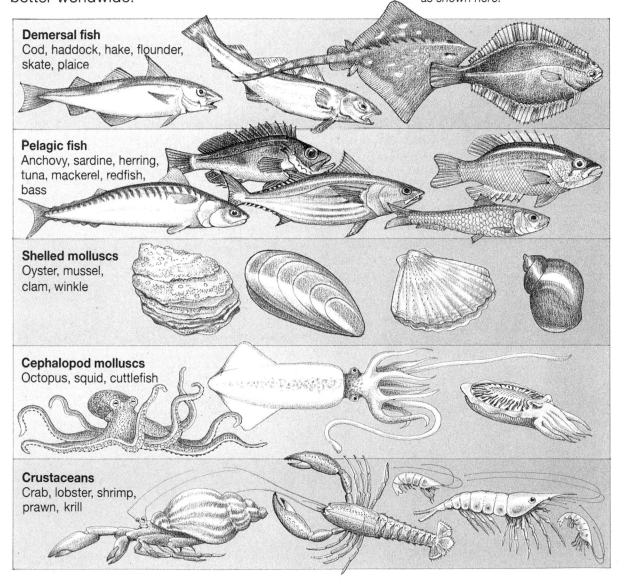

Demersal fish
Cod, haddock, hake, flounder, skate, plaice

Pelagic fish
Anchovy, sardine, herring, tuna, mackerel, redfish, bass

Shelled molluscs
Oyster, mussel, clam, winkle

Cephalopod molluscs
Octopus, squid, cuttlefish

Crustaceans
Crab, lobster, shrimp, prawn, krill

CLEANING UP RIVERS

The mighty river Rhine and its many tributaries run through four countries in Europe. They provide water for drinking, industry, transport, agriculture and wine-growing. Tens of millions of people depend on the river for their livelihoods. By 1970, the river was seriously polluted. The countries sharing its waters decided that action was needed. Towns along its banks contributed many millions of pounds for the clean-up. By 1985 fish, shrimps and other animals were back.

However, accidents happen. At 1am on 1 November 1986, a fire broke out in a chemical warehouse near the Rhine at Basel, Switzerland (shown on the map). While the fire was being put out, 30 tonnes of poisonous agricultural chemicals were hosed into the river. There was a 10-hour delay before warnings went out that poisoned water was flowing down to the sea.

AGREEMENTS

In 1990, European governments agreed to cut the discharges of 37 dangerous chemicals into the North Sea, by 50% within five years. Over the same time period, they also aim to reduce by 70% the discharges of four poisonous chemicals – cadmium, mercury, lead and dioxin.

GETTING BETTER
The River Rhine was slowly recovering its health during the early 1980s (left). By about 1985, its eels were again safe to eat. The accident at Basel put back this recovery by many years (right).

A "FIRST"

In 1989, Shell UK pumped water through a broken pipeline into the River Mersey, in England, to flush out oil and save the pipeline. The 450-kilometre oil slick killed 300 birds, and harmed water animals. Shell were prosecuted in the first case for the UK's new National Rivers Authority, the "pollution police".

SPILLED OIL
Sometimes pipelines like this one in Alaska (see right) break. The spilled oil can pollute the sea and rivers over a wide area. There have been significant leakages from drilling rigs off the Southern Californian coast. The chemicals used to clean up these spills have done as much damage as the oil.

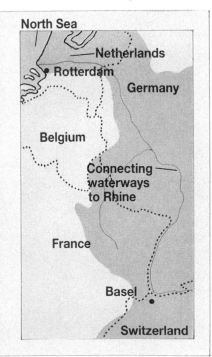

Towns brought in tankers of water from other places. The Dutch saved Isselmeer Lake by directing the poisoned water into the North Sea. The poisons were much diluted, but they still damaged sea life, and many thousands of fish were killed. The accident left behind 250 kilometres of dead river.

Laws to control and cut down water pollution have been introduced slowly. Even when there are laws, industry is often able to break them without being punished. In the Humber Estuary of North East England, 1500 pipelines pour toxic waste and sewage into the river. From 1985 to 1989, Britain's already slack pollution laws were broken nearly 300 times – in this one estuary. There were only a handful of prosecutions.

Matters are slowly improving. Some Scandinavian countries want laws to prevent all industrial pollution of rivers by the end of the century. This policy is called "Zero emissions". It would make factories use less dangerous chemicals, produce less waste, and recycle those wastes as much as possible.

SAVING THE SEAS

In shallow and relatively enclosed seas, such as the North Sea and the Mediterranean, the waters are particularly at risk. They suffer from sewage discharges as well as pollution from the land brought in by rivers.

The Mediterranean is a worrying example of how bad this kind of pollution can become. Much of the northern coastline, and some of its African coastline, is the "summer playground" of European holidaymakers. Tourism is worth billions of pounds to the countries around its shores. Yet these same countries pour billions of litres of raw sewage into the Mediterranean each year. Minor illnesses such as sickness and diarrhoea are common, and there are risks of more serious diseases. The tourist trade is endangered by pollution in a growing number of areas.

Industries add to the Mediterranean's load. Industrial and domestic waste from many rivers, some very large, eventually find their way into the Mediterranean

NORTH ATLANTIC

Although enclosed seas are most at risk from pollution, large open seas like the Pacific and Atlantic are also under threat. For example, toxic sewage is discharged into the sea around New Jersey (see page 27). Yearly waste discharges into the New York Bight (thousand tonnes) are as follows:

Carbon	949
Oil compounds	318
Nitrates	190
Copper	5
Lead	4.6
Mercury	0.1
PCBs	0.005

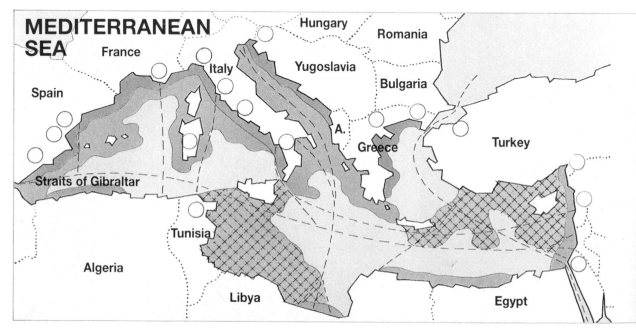

MEDITERRANEAN SEA

France
Spain
Italy
Straits of Gibraltar
Tunisia
Algeria
Libya
Hungary
Romania
Yugoslavia
Bulgaria
A.
Greece
Turkey
Egypt

Sea or the Black Sea. Another major problem is oil tankers which wash out their tanks at sea, deliberately and illegally spilling oil into the water.

Not much of this pollution moves out of the enclosed sea. Most of the year, water flows into the Mediterranean from the Atlantic Ocean. Only in the winter does some water travel back to the Atlantic, along the sea bed through the Straits of Gibraltar. So the current levels of pollution will take many years to fall, even if all discharges stop tomorrow.

CENTRES OF POLLUTION
In the Mediterranean, the heaviest oil pollution is along the coasts of Libya and Tunisia, at the sites where oil is loaded on to ships (see left). Around 25% of the world's oil pollution occurs in enclosed waters such as the Mediterranean.

TOURIST TRAP
Areas like the Greek Islands (below) have become popular as holiday resorts. This causes huge problems as many of these countries cannot cope with the increased sewage and pollution. The same problems are now becoming evident in tourist areas in the South Pacific.

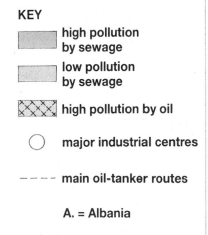

KEY

high pollution by sewage

low pollution by sewage

high pollution by oil

○ major industrial centres

- - - - main oil-tanker routes

A. = Albania

SAVING SEA LIFE

Stone Age people hunted for fish and other water animals with traps, nets and spears. Whales were hunted at least 1000 years ago. There were fewer people then, and their whaling techniques were less efficient, so few whales were killed.

Modern people continued whaling, but with new techniques. They easily kill animals as large as the blue whale and unintentionally catch in their nets whales as small as dolphins and porpoises. The result? Many types of sea animals are in danger of extinction.

For example, Juan Fernandez fur seals used to number millions, but are now down to around 1500. The numbers of blue whales have dropped from about 200,000 to only 11,000. The blue whale weighs up to 136 tonnes and is bigger than the largest dinosaur ever was. It is in danger of following the dinosaurs into extinction. But it would be a man-made extinction, not a natural one. If we do not stop hunting marine mammals, we may lose some of them for ever.

DISAPPEARING WHALES

There are about 84 species of whales (cetaceans), which include dolphins and porpoises. They are warm-blooded and breathe air, just like other mammals, so they must surface regularly to take in air. Whales show complex social behaviour. They play, care for their young, and protect each other. Their numbers have been devastated by whaling, accidental trapping in nets, and killing to protect the fish stocks which they are supposed to eat.

The Fin Whale, Blue Whale, Sei Whale and Humpback Whale (see right) have all suffered from overhunting. It will take many years for the numbers to increase, if ever. They may be doomed to extinction.

WHAT ARE MARINE MAMMALS?

There are three main groups of marine, or sea-living, mammals. These are the whales, the seals (see below), walruses and sealions, and the much rarer seacows (dugongs and manatees).

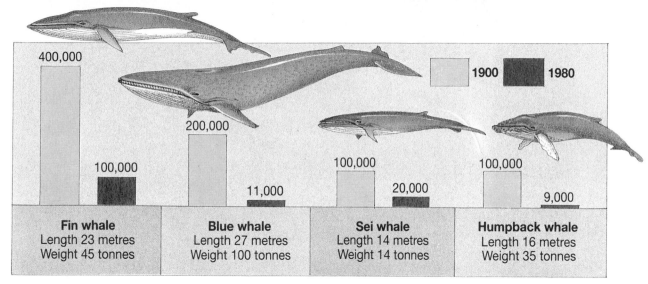

	1900		1980

Fin whale
Length 23 metres
Weight 45 tonnes

400,000
100,000

Blue whale
Length 27 metres
Weight 100 tonnes

200,000
11,000

Sei whale
Length 14 metres
Weight 14 tonnes

100,000
20,000

Humpback whale
Length 16 metres
Weight 35 tonnes

100,000
9,000

From 1986, most countries agreed to stop whaling. The only countries that objected to the ban were Japan, Iceland, the USSR and Norway. Since 1986, they have killed thousands of whales. They claim that they are killing whales for "research purposes". Meanwhile, Japanese restaurants continue to sell whale meat.

Pollution is also a danger to marine mammals. Toxic chemicals from the food they eat are concentrated in the layer of fatty blubber just below the skin. These chemicals are linked to malformed offspring in birds and mammals.

DROWNED AT SEA

Sea mammals like these Pacific Bottlenose dolphins found off the coast of the USA and Japan are sometimes killed because they get caught in drift nets – fine nets laid down over many kilometres which are used to catch fish such as tuna. Dolphins and porpoises cannot see the thin but strong mesh. They are drawn to the nets by the struggling fish, which they view as a good meal.

PROTECT OUR WATER

Gulf of Alaska

Canada

USA

Alaska

Many abuses of the world's waters could be avoided if people took more care. For those who say we already take enough care, the *Exxon Valdez* disaster in 1989 is a clear example that we don't.

In the first few minutes of Easter Monday, 1989, the large oil-tanker *Exxon Valdez* ran aground on rocks, about 40 kilometres from the oil terminal of Valdez, Alaska. It had been taking on crude oil at the port. The night was clear but the tanker was outside its shipping lane, which is some 16 kilometres wide.

Valdez Marine Terminal

Bligh Reef
(site of tanker
grounding)

Montague Island

KEY

■ oil slick

← shipping lanes

OIL DISASTER
The Exxon Valdez (see left) ran aground spilling its cargo of oil. The coastline of Alaska and its wildlife were smothered in oil.

The sailors on the ship called the Coastguard 23 minutes later. By then, one-eighth of their cargo was smeared over the sea. Coastguards estimate that one-fifth – almost 50,000 cubic metres – was lost by noon. A week later, that one-fifth had spread over some 2400 square kilometres of sea in Prince William Sound. Storms mixed it into a thick "mousse" of water and oil. This soon became very difficult to clear from the water and the contaminated beaches.

More than 1300 kilometres of coast, and 4800 square kilometres of water, were affected by the spillage. Wild-life deaths were counted in tens of thousands. Many sea birds and sea otters died at once, smothered in oil. Many more animals died slower deaths including deer, bears and bald eagles, which take food from the beach. Herring fishing was stopped for a year. Salmon fisheries were also badly affected. One of the cleanest remaining parts of the Earth's oceans suffered environmental catastrophe. It will take years to recover.

HOW DID IT HAPPEN?

Preliminary findings suggest that there were several possible contributions to the *Exxon Valdez* accident.

● The ship was poorly handled; some of the crew were not at their positions, and some were not in a fit state for work.

● The Coastguard did not act immediately when the ship first started wandering off course.

● The oil companies' agents, responsible for dealing with oil spills, took longer to act than they should, and essential equipment was unavailable.

● Attempts to clean up the oil were not sufficient, and not completed properly .

● An oil terminal allowing safer tanker control should have been built, but the main oil companies using Port Valdez said it would be too expensive.

THE WRONG OIL
Sea birds and mammals rely on natural oils in their feathers and fur. The oil helps waterproofing, which keeps in body warmth and enables the animal to float. Crude oil destroys this. The oiled animal either freezes, drowns or starves. These seabirds were found on the Dutch coastline covered with grease and oil. Without help they would die.

STOP THE DUMPING

MENDING THEIR WAYS

We have no exact information on many of the chemicals dumped into rivers, lakes and seas. We do not know what they will do to the creatures and plants that live in the water or drink it. Industry is allowed to continue dumping its wastes until there is firm evidence of harm.

This is the wrong approach. By the time scientists can point to firm evidence of harm, the damage has been done. It is too late for the wildlife and the people that depend on the water. Even when there is evidence of harm, industries find it easy to persuade the government that there is no real problem. They say: "Dilution is the solution to pollution." The governments give them permission to reduce the amount of toxins, rather than stop them altogether. Again, this is wrong. Nature simply cannot deal with so many chemicals and make them harmless. Levels of toxins rise.

It is not all doom and gloom. Progress is being made. In 1987, European governments promised to end dumping of liquid industrial waste by 1989. All countries did so – except Britain, which announced that it would carry on until 1992.

In many countries some companies continue throwing away their liquid wastes and toxins until they are forced to stop, by law. These are a few of the liquid waste discharges, allowed each year in the UK which should be stopped by 1990-92.
- 45,000 tonnes on Tyneside from Sterling Organics (42,000 tonnes) and Orsynetics (3,000 tonnes).
- More than 170,000 tonnes on Teeside from ICI (165,000 tonnes) and Fine Organics (8,000 tonnes).
- More than 17,000 tonnes from Allied Colloids (15,000 tonnes), Woolcombers (999 tonnes) and Chlor-Chem (1000 tonnes).
- 33,000 tonnes on the Thames from Tate & Lyle.

ADOPT THE PRECAUTIONARY PRINCIPLE

This principle says: if we do not know whether a chemical harms the environment, then it should not be released. In other words, give the benefit of the doubt to the environment, not to industry. The law must say: "If you don't know what it does, don't dump it."

Factory outflows like this one from a pulp and paper factory in Huelva, Spain must be stopped. If the bleaches and chemicals used in the process escape into the rivers and seas they can damage plant and animal life.

REDUCE POLLUTION AND RESTORE LAND

Industry should also restore land after use, such as here in West Germany. Earth removed during mining is being replaced and the land restored for agricultural use. They should also spend more on reducing pollution at source. Manufacturing processes must produce less waste and toxins to start with, rather than making lots of wastes and toxins and then having to treat them.

AIM FOR "ZERO DISCHARGES"

The incinerator ship Vesta, from West Germany (see right), burned thousands of tonnes of toxic waste and dumped the remains at sea. Public pressure finally caused this ship to stop operating in December 1989.

All governments should adopt the goal of Denmark, which is aiming at zero discharge from its industries. Factories should not be allowed to throw away wastes and dangerous chemicals, and forget about them – making nature do their dirty work.

STOP THE POLLUTION

We are all responsible for helping to stop pollution. Take your rubbish home, or put it in a bin – do not just drop it and destroy the countryside. On a wider scale governments must give their pollution officers more powers. The polluters should expect proper punishment and stiff fines. This means more staff and resources for the monitoring and control of pollution.

HOW WE CAN ALL HELP

The way we live is causing many of the environmental problems that our Earth faces. There are lots of little things we can do that, when added together, make a big difference.

For example, if every person in the industrialized countries used a tap for just one minute less each day, then billions of litres of water would be saved. It would save on drawing water from rivers and reservoirs, on pumping it from groundwater supplies, on cleaning and purifying it before use, and on treating it after use in drainage and sewage plants.

There are many other things that we can do, which are similarly useful. Here are a few. Can you get together with your friends or at school, and think of others? Remember that you, and your children, will inherit what is happening now. Some older people and some companies have no thought for the future – they have already taken what they want. They are leaving you to deal with the mess. Remember that our Earth's waters are in trouble. They need everyone's help.

OUT AND ABOUT

● Look out for pollution in rivers, lakes and the sea. If you find any, report it

● Write politely to the local council and regional water company, and tell them about pollution

● Try to find who is causing pollution. If you find out, write to them. A polite letter from a young person can have more effect than a letter from an adult

● Take your litter home or put it in litter bins. Do not throw it into the water

● Avoid beaches contaminated with sewage or oil. Write to your local council, to explain why. Encourage other people to do the same

AROUND THE HOUSE

There are many ways to reduce the amount of water we use.

● Wash the car using a bucket, not a hose

● Pour dirty washing-up water on the garden to water the plants, instead of using a sprinkler

● Take showers instead of baths

● Don't pour oil, cleaning fluids or paint down the drain

● Use as little plastic as possible. Never burn it – burning plastic can put toxic dioxins into the air, which find their way into water supplies

USE PUBLIC INFORMATION

● In many countries, polluters have to admit their actions in official documents

● In Britain the Water Authorities Public Registers give lists of pollution. In the USA, the Freedom of Information Act can be used to get information on pollution

● Polluters rely on people not understanding these kinds of documents, and on governments turning a blind eye. Show them that they are wrong

● Be an environmental detective. Find out who is causing the pollution and write to them or get up a petition asking them to stop

LET PEOPLE KNOW

● Write to those who deal with sewage and rubbish collection. Ask how it is treated

● Raw sewage should not be put into the sea or rivers. If companies or people are doing this, ask why. Are they outside the law?

● Ask for collection points for glass bottles, paper, oil and cleaning fluids

● Make your local and national representatives, such as councillors and MPs, aware of your views. Tell them you are the voters of the future, and you want a clean, safe world to live in

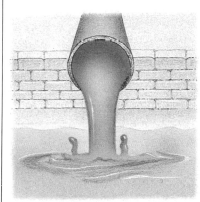

GET INVOLVED

● Support an environmental group. They are trying to care for the world you will spend your life in

● Help to raise funds for environmental projects by sponsored events or collections

● Write to the local papers whenever you find that water is being mistreated. If they are not interested, ask why. Shouldn't they be reporting important damage to our surroundings?

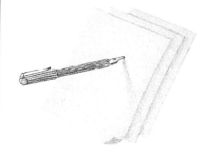

IN THE SHOPS

● Avoid buying plastic. Look for glass bottles, paper wrappings and re-useable containers that can be recycled

● Buy detergent powders and liquids that are free from phosphates

● Try to use shops that sell environment-friendly products, even if they are slightly more expensive. As a consumer, you have great power to change the way industries think

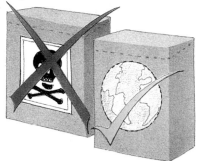

GLOSSARY

Acid rain   Rain, dew or snow which is more acidic than is natural. Acid rain is produced when sulphur dioxide and nitrogen oxide gases, given off when fossil fuels like coal and oil are burned, combine with rain water. Acid rain can damage buildings, plants and animals.

Bio-accumulation   Concentrations of a particular toxic substance can build up progressively in animals' tissues. When one animal is eaten by another, a toxic chemical can become even more concentrated in the second animal's tissues. In this way, the chemicals slowly build up in the animals' tissues until they can cause death.

Dehydration   When a substance, a plant or an animal lacks water which it needs, it is suffering from dehydration.

Eutrophication   A process that results from pollution when too much phosphate and nitrate drains into rivers, lakes and seas. Phosphate and nitrate, which come from fertilizers and detergents for example, are nutrients for algae (microscopic plants). Because there is so much phosphate and nitrate, algae grow very quickly, forming a "bloom" in the water. The algal bloom uses up oxygen which other plants and animals need in order to live in the water. In some cases, eutrophication goes so far that it makes the water unfit for the growth of any animals or plants.

Greenhouse effect   The trapping in the atmosphere of infrared (heat) radiation from the Earth's surface. Greenhouse gases such as carbon dioxide, which are produced when fuels such as coal, oil and wood are burned, do this.

HHCs   Toxic chemicals, called halogenated hydrocarbons, which are made by combining halogens (like chlorine) with hydrocarbons (substances, such as oil, are made of hydrogen and carbon).

Irrigation   The provision of water to an area where there would not normally be enough to make crops grow.

Nutrients   The chemicals and minerals, such as phosphates and nitrates, that are taken up by the roots of plants, or taken in by animals as food. They are essential for the growth of living things.

PCBs   A group of HHCs, called polychlorinated biphenyls, whose main characteristic is that they are resistant to heat. They have been banned from production since 1981 because of their toxicity, but are still to be found in many electrical insulation products around the world.

Precipitation   When water condenses and falls as rain, snow or hail.

Transpiration   The passage of water up through a plant. Water is drawn in by the roots and evaporated from the leaves.

FURTHER READING

For Children
Pollution and the Environment by M. Lean; MacDonald Children's Books, 1985.
Water Ecology by J. Cochrane; Project Ecology, Wayland, 1987.
The Dying Sea by M. Bright; Franklin Watts, 1988.
Pollution and Conservation by Malcolm Penny; Wayland, 1988.
War on Waste by P. Neal; Dryad Press, 1989.
Acid Rain by J. Baines; Conserving Our World, Wayland, 1989.

For Adults
The Gaia Atlas of Planet Management by N. Myers (editor); Pan Books, 1985.
Ecology Facts by M. Allaby; Hamlyn, 1986.
The Earth Report by E. Goldsmith and N. Hildyard (editors); Mitchell Beazely, 1990.

USEFUL ADDRESSES

Department of the Environment (DoE)
2, Marsham Street, London SW1
The DoE has many leaflets and guidelines on environmental issues.

Council for Environmental Education
School of Education, University of Reading, London Road, Reading, Berks RG1 5AQ
Helps youth organizations to learn more about the environment.

Friends of the Earth (FoE)
26–28 Underwood Street, London N1
FoE is an action group that organizes campaigns on environmental issues. They have a youth section, Earth Action, for people aged 14 to 23.

Greenpeace UK
30–31 Islington Green, London N1 8XE
Greenpeace organizes protests and campaigns against the destruction of the environment. They also present scientific information on various environmental projects to many governments. They will answer questions and give advice to organizations and schoolchildren who write to them.

Marine Conservation Society
9 Gloucester Road, Ross on Wye, Herefordshire HR9 5BU.
This society works to conserve the oceans and all their inhabitants.

Waste Watch
National Council for Voluntary Organizations, 26 Bedford Square, London WC1B 3HU.
Details of local environmental groups and voluntary organizations in the UK are available from Waste Watch.

WATCH Trust for Environmental Education Ltd
22 The Green, Nettleham, Lincoln LN2 2NR
WATCH works with schools and helps to organize conservation projects. It aims to increase knowledge of the natural world and encourage conservation.

World Wide Fund for Nature (WWF)
Panda House, Weyside Park, Godalming, Surrey GU7 1XR
WWF encourages the conservation of plants and animals throughout the world.

INDEX